W9-AJN-154

SOCIAL STUDIES

MACMILLAN

Macmillan Social Studies

THE UNITED STATES AND THE OTHER AMERICAS

SENIOR AUTHOR
John Jarolimek

Allen Y. King
Ida Dennis
Florence Potter

GEOGRAPHY CONSULTANT
Loyal Durand, Jr.

Macmillan Publishing Company
New York

Collier Macmillan Publishers
London

Parts of this book were published in earlier editions of
Macmillan Social Studies.

Macmillan Publishing Company
866 Third Avenue, New York, New York 10022
Collier Macmillan Canada, Inc.

Printed in the United States of America
ISBN 0-02-147380-3
9 8 7 6 5 4 3 2

Acknowledgments

The publisher gratefully acknowledges permission to reprint the following
copyrighted material:

Excerpt from article on Jane Addams and excerpt from article on John
Cabot: Reprinted with permission of the *New Book of Knowledge,*
copyright © 1983, Grolier Inc.
Excerpt from *A Child's Geography of the World* by V. M. Hillyer and
E. G. Huey. Copyright 1929 by the Century Company; copyright 1951
by Appleton-Century-Crofts, Inc.; copyright 1957 by Mercantile Safe
Deposit and Trust Co. Reprinted by permission of E.P. Dutton, Inc.

Cover:
Illustration by Robert LoGrippo

Maps:
Joe LeMonnier and Bielat Studios, Chris Ellithorpe, Robert Forget, Yvette
Heyden, Liska and Associates, Cathy Meindl, Jeff Mellander, Jay Songero,
Lowell Stumpf, George Suyeoka, John Walter & Associates. Map Skills
developed and produced by Educational Challenges, Inc., Alexandria, VA.

Illustrations:
Dev Appleyard, Yoshi Miyake, Tak Murakami, Alexis Oussenko,
Hima Pamoedjo

Photographs:
Abbot Hall, Marblehead, Ma.: Original of this painting hangs in the
Selectmen's Room, 69
Courtesy of American Heritage Pub. Co., Inc.:
Collection of Christopher Reed, 88; Nebraska State Historical Society,
Soloman D. Butcher Collection, 181
American Museum of Natural History, courtesy of the Library Services
Department: 25 center left, top and bottom right, 37, 39 detail, 50, 326
Art Resource: Scala, 44, 477, Joseph Martin, National Portrait Gallery,
Washington, D.C., 579 bottom right, Historical Society of Pennsylvania,

170; Snark International, 215 center right, The Library of Congress, 191;
© Peter Vadnai, 218 bottom
Atoz/Van Cleve: © Betty Crowell, 346
The Bettmann Archive, Inc.: 31, 43, 62 top, 74, 77 top right, 107, 117 left
center, 178, 195, 200, 202, 207, 231, 302, 303, 384, 415, 419, 549, 571,
Photograph by Lewis Hine, 193
Black Star Publishing Co., Inc.: © Brad Hess, 556; © Ernest R. Manewal,
403; © Bill Ray, 215 top left; © Fred Ward, 489; © Doug Wilson, 13
© Lee Boltin: 40
Brown Bros: 267, 347, 350
California State Library, Sacramento: Photograph Collection, 411, 551
© Cameramann Int., Inc.: 288 top, 296, 322, 330, 332, 335, 336, 343, 349
right, 367 bottom, 369, 394, 439, 440, 442 bottom left and right, 443,
482, 497
Courtesy CBS, Inc.: 77 center right
Chicago Historical Society: 166 bottom
Cities Service: 363 left
Colour Library International: 63 center right and bottom
The Connecticut Historical Society: 540
© J. Dan Coop: 354 bottom
© Martha Cooper: 533
In the Collection of the Corcoran Gallery of Art: J.P. Newell; *Lazell, Perkins
& Co. Bridgewater, Mass., Manufacturers of all Descriptions of Forgings
for Steam-Ships and Rail-Roads, Castings and all Kinds of Machinery*;
Museum Purchase, Mary E. Maxwell Fund, 166 top
Culver Pictures, Inc.: 146, 163, 210, 233, 268, 422
The Department of the Treasury: 232
© Greg Dorata: 24 bottom
Eastern National Park & Monument Association, 106
Courtesy Fraunces Tavern Museum, New York City, 96
© Freeport Sulphur: 363 right
Gamma Liaison: © Charlon, 214 center; © Dirck Halstead, 214 top and
bottom

Continued on page 600

CONTENTS

Maps

Diagrams, Charts, and Graphs

ATLAS

THE WORLD
POLITICAL

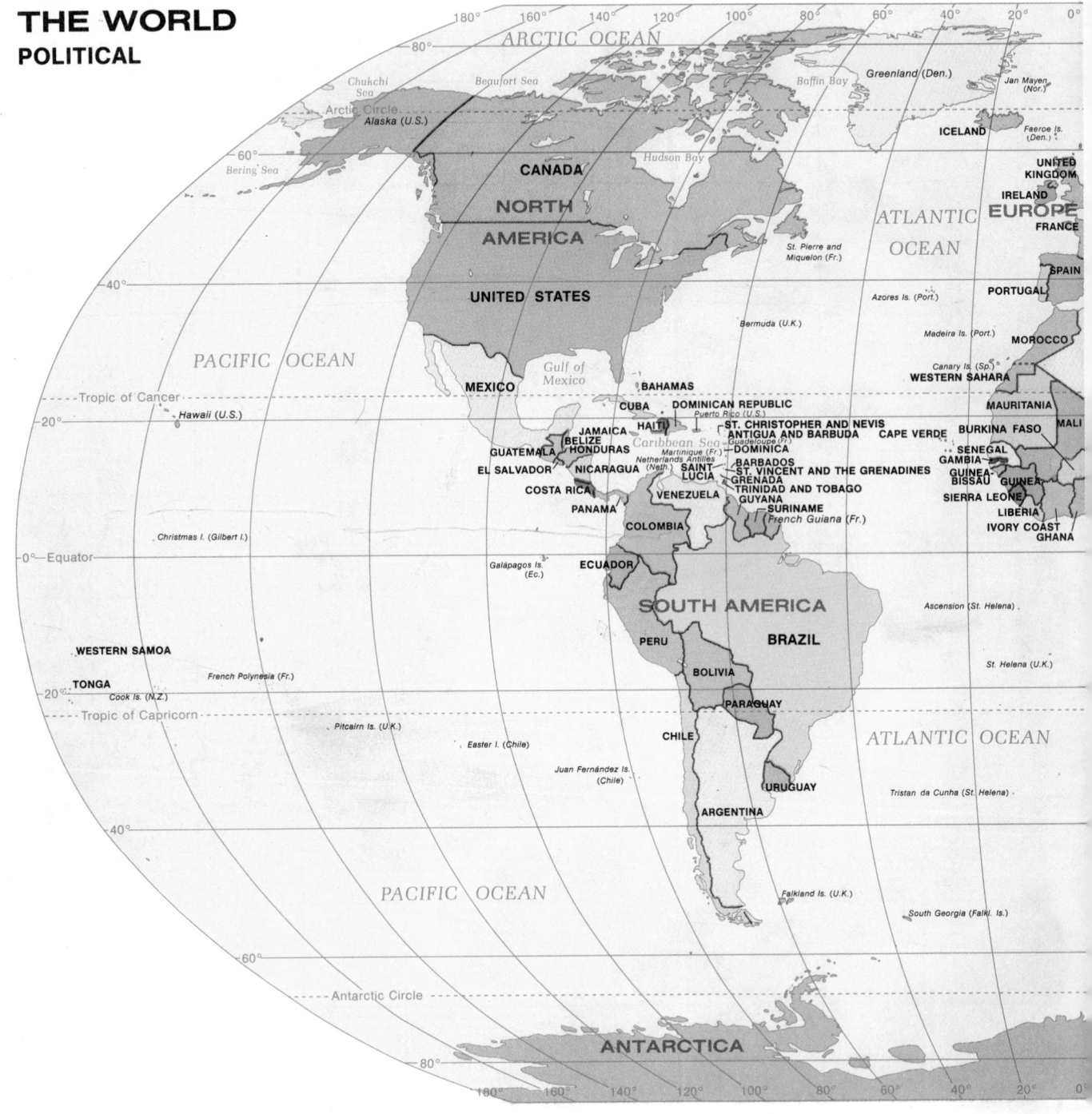

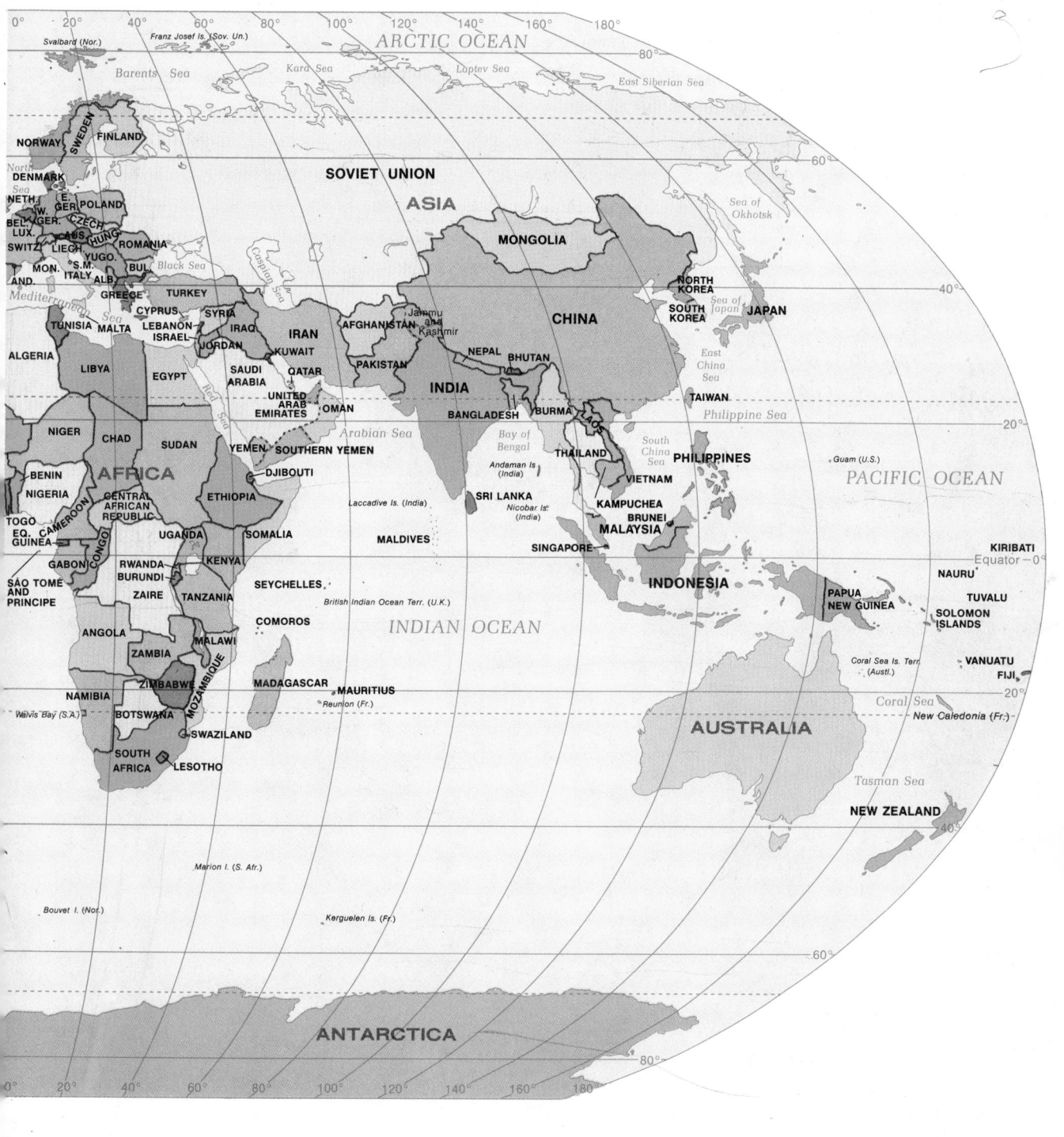

ALB. = ALBANIA	**LIECH.** = LIECHTENSTEIN
AND. = ANDORRA	**LUX.** = LUXEMBOURG
AUS. = AUSTRIA	**MON.** = MONACO
BEL. = BELGIUM	**NETH.** = NETHERLANDS
BUL. = BULGARIA	**S.M.** = SAN MARINO
CZECH. = CZECHOSLOVAKIA	**SWITZ.** = SWITZERLAND
E.GER. = EAST GERMANY	**W.GER.** = WEST GERMANY
HUNG. = HUNGARY	**YUGO.** = YUGOSLAVIA

A-3